Crockle A

Written and Illustrated by

John Ryan

One hot summer day Mrs Noah came out on to the deck of the Ark to try on a fine new straw sun-hat which Mrs Ham had made for her.

The family, and the animals who were out there, thought it was beautiful

and Mr Noah agreed with them.

Even gloomy Mrs Shem said she liked it,

and Shem, who looked after the money and could only think how expensive the things for making the hat must have been, did his best to smile.

Cheerful Ham the ship's carpenter was very proud of Mrs Ham.

Jaffet, Mr Noah's youngest son, and his friend Jannet liked the hat too.

Gosh!

Could you make one for me, Mrs Ham?

Crockle the baby crocodile had another idea. He belonged to the children and shouldn't have been on the Ark at all . . .

because there were already two perfectly good (or bad) cracodiles on board.

When Crockle saw Mrs Noah's hat he thought it might fit *him* rather well.

Just then Mrs Noah remembered a cake which she had left in the oven.

But when she ran in, her hat was too big, and got stuck in the door,

so she took it off and put it down on the handrail of the Ark

and ran indoors to look after her cake.

When she came back a little later she had a shock. Crockle had decided that her hat was just right for him. Only *not* on his head.

Mrs Noah was cross. She shouted at Crockle, who turned round so suddenly . . .

that the hat started to spin like a top.

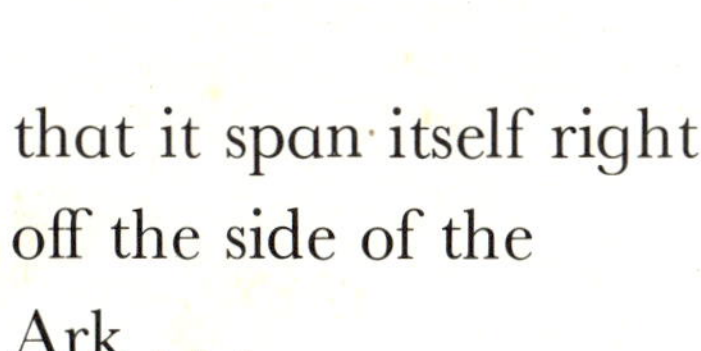

It went so fast . . .

that it span itself right off the side of the Ark . . .

and landed with a big SPLASH in the water below.

Then Mrs Noah's hat with Crockle still in it began to drift quite quickly away from the Ark.

When they saw what had happened the children were very anxious.

But Ham said, 'Don't worry! We'll go after him in the dinghy.' 'Oh please can we row it?' asked Jaffet, 'It's our fault really, because he is *our* pet crocodile!'

'What do you think father?' said Ham. Mr Noah looked at the water. 'The water's smooth enough,' he said. 'They'll be quite safe . . .

‘as long as they wear life jackets.’ So Shem and Ham lowered the dinghy and Jaffet and Jannet climbed into it.

Then each of the children took an oar. They were quite good at rowing and it wasn't long before they caught up with Crockle and pulled him, hat and all, safely on board.

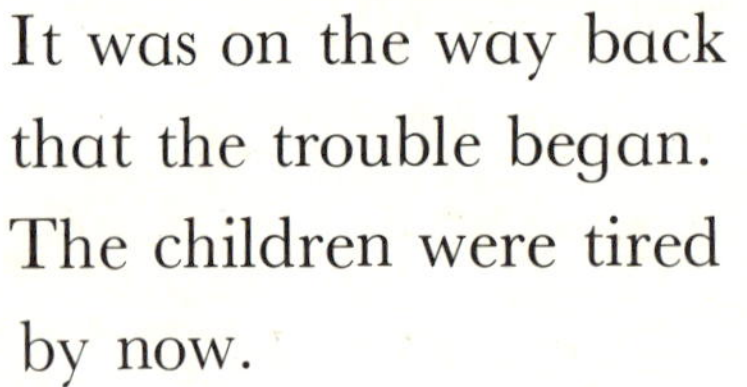

It was on the way back that the trouble began. The children were tired by now.

Suddenly Jaffet let his oar slip, and a moment later . . .

he was on his back in the bottom of the boat.

Jaffet was all right but his oar was gone. Already it had drifted too far to reach.

The children knew they mustn't go in the water because of all the fierce creatures that lived there.

'How can we get back to the Ark with only one oar?' asked Jannet. 'I don't know,' said Jaffet, 'but we'll try . . .

'only it does look a very long way!'

On board the Ark everybody could see what was happening.

They watched the little boat going round in circles

as Jaffet did his best to row back with one oar.

But the boat seemed to get further away, not nearer. 'If they can't get back to us we'll have to take the Ark over to them,' said Shem. 'Easier said than done, brother,' replied Ham.

'We don't even know which end is the front!'

‘Which *is* the front, father?’ he asked.

‘I don’t know,’ said Mr Noah. ‘But it doesn’t make much difference. We haven’t even got anything to use as a sail.’

‘But the children have!’ cried Mrs Noah. ‘They could use my hat!’ ‘Now that *is* a good idea,’ said Mr Noah. ‘Let’s tell them!’

So the family all lined up and shouted to the children. The animals did their best to join in too.

'What's that they're calling?' asked Jaffet. 'Sounds like "Who's as fat as a whale?" to me,' said Jannet.

'Or "Puss-cat in the pail",' said Jaffet. Then they noticed Crockle.

He was making funny grunting noises and thumping the hat with his front paws. 'Why of course!' cried Jannet.

‘They want us to use the hat as a sail.’

But first they had to get Crockle out of the hat. It wasn’t easy. Crockle had a fat tummy and the hat had shrunk in the water.

So Jannet took the hat and Jaffet took Crockle, and they both tugged . . .
and tugged . . .
and tugged . . .
until . . .

Crockle and the hat were parted at last.

'Just in time too,' said Jannet. 'Look at those nasty black clouds coming up on the horizon.' 'Come on then,' said Jaffet. 'You hold the hat and I'll steer.'

And away they went. Crockle helped Jannet with the hat and luckily there was just enough breeze to blow them along, and what was more . . .

to blow them in the right direction.

‘Blow harder wind!’ called Jaffet. ‘It’s going to rain soon!’ And the wind did blow, but of course that brought the black clouds closer. So that they just had time to get to the missing oar and pick it up . . .

and then sail back to the Ark before the rain started.

Ham was ready for
them and very soon . . .

they were all safely back on deck again.

Of course Mrs Noah was very pleased to get her new hat back, even if it was a bit wet.

That evening there was a special high tea because it had been such an adventurous day. And although he *had* been rather naughty, Mrs Ham made Crockle a new hat too. It was just right for size . . . only this time

he wore it on the right end!